RABBI ROCKETPOWER

A TOOTY FRUITY
FOR TU BISHVAT
A JUICY MYSTERY

WRITTEN BY
RABBI SUSAN ABRAMSON

ILLUSTRATED BY
LAURA STANDLEY

OAK LEAF SYSTEMS

MASSACHUSETTS   VIRGINIA

Copyright © 2011

by
Susan Abramson

**Rabbi Rocketpower
In A
Tooty Fruity Tale For Tu Bishvat -
A Juicy Mystery**

by Rabbi Susan Abramson

Illustrations by Laura Standley

~ ~ ~ ~ ~

First Printing

November 2011

Library of Congress Catalog Card Number: pending
ISBN: 978-0-9659546-8-6

Published by:
Oak Leaf Systems   Massachusetts   Virginia

~ ~ ~ ~ ~

A portion of the profits from this book
will be donated to charity.

www.rabbirocketpower.com
Printed on Recycled Paper

We've got to get ourselves back to the garden.

-Joni Mitchell

I've gt to gt myslf bck to Th Grdn.

-Tooty Fruity

ABOUT THE AUTHOR

Rabbi Susan Abramson is a graduate of Brandeis University and Hebrew Union College – Jewish Institute of Religion. She received her Doctor of Divinity degree from Hebrew Union College in 2006.

She has been the rabbi of Temple Shalom Emeth in Burlington, Massachusetts since 1984.

ABOUT THE ILLUSTRATOR

Laura Standley is a senior at Woburn Memorial High School and an active member of Temple Shalom Emeth. She will be pursuing a career in engineering, and she hopes to minor in art in college.

CONTENTS

A Juicy Tu Bishvat History Mystery

MY FAMILY TREE
DAD
A brilliant computer scientist. He speaks many languages and can find any information you want on his awesome secret supercomputer.
MOM
Rabbi Beatrice A. Mensch (B. A. Mensch for short). She can turn into the fearless Rabbi Rocketpower. She shouts, "Oy vay, up, up, and away!" when she flies off to save the day.
ME
Superboy in training. I'm the first to spot trouble. I'm my mother's right hand boy. I help save the day!
PURR
Our cat. Her real name is Purreneal Pest. She's from the planet P.I.A., which stands for "Pain in the asteroid.
You won't believe what happened at this year's seder. Stick around and you'll find out!
WHO YOU CALLIN' A STICK?!

CHAPTER ONE

TU BISH WHAT?

Aaron zoomed into the kitchen, still wearing his school backpack. "Purr, please get your nose out of that bowl of raisins," he shouted.

All he could see was Purr's tail and everything that was attached to it sticking up in the air on the kitchen table. She was sniffing inside a big glass bowl.

"If you people think I'm gonna eat this yucky brown wrinkly cat food, you're nuts," Purr huffed.

"That's not cat food!" Aaron exclaimed. "It's raisins that we're bringing to the *temple* for our *Tu Bishvat seder*."

"Speaking of nuts," added Rabbi Mensch, as she poured another box of raisins into the bowl, "we're going to eat them at the *seder*, too."

"Don't tell me you melon heads are having another Jewish holiday." Purr rolled her eyes. "Hey, maybe you could name this one after me. You could call it Tu BishPurr. Then maybe I could decide what I want to eat for a change. Let's see. I think I'll start with the leaves from the plant in the living room, then the mouse that I caught running down the chimney last night..."

"*Tu Bishvat* is the holiday when we thank G-d for nature. We're supposed to think about all the ways we need to take care of it, not torture it," Aaron interrupted, not wanting to think about what might have happened to that poor mouse. "It means the 15th day of the Jewish month called *Shvat*. It's the New Year for the Trees and the beginning of spring in Israel."

"What if I spring into a real big bowl of catnip? Now that would be worth having a holiday about," she suggested.

"We're supposed to drink four cups of wine or grape juice in honor of the four seasons of the year. Then we eat three different types of fruit, preferably the kind you find in Israel," explained Rabbi Mensch, ignoring Purr's comment as she and Aaron poured more raisins into the bowl.

"We eat fruit with outer shells, like oranges, pomegranates or almonds; fruit with pits, like dates or olives; and fruit that you can eat all of, like figs or grapes or these raisins. We try to eat the *seven types of fruit* from Israel. Some people even eat 15 different fruits in honor of it being the 15th day of the month."

"If catnip ain't a fruit then I ain't interested," Purr announced. "I think I'll take a little Tu Bish Nap. Wake me up when it's over."

"Just don't sleep on the windowsill again please," Aaron requested. "Every time you see a squirrel in the backyard, you dream about chasing them and wag your tail so hard that it knocks all the plants onto the floor."

"Squirrels, shmirrels." Purr yawned. "I'm too tired to jump all the way up there anyway."

She stepped onto a thin black metal box next to the bowl of raisins and curled up in a ball.

CHAPTER TWO

TU BISH WHAT-CHAMACALLIT

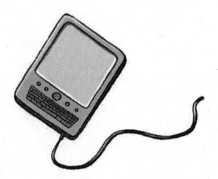

Rabbi Mensch shooed Purr onto the floor. "Purr, get off of there right now!" she yelled.

"What happened?" asked Aaron, nearly dropping another box of raisins.

"Purr was about to take a nap on Dad's brand new invention," she explained. "I'm charging the battery so we can use it at the temple this evening. It's called the *Time-Warp-Turbo-History-5772-XL*."

"The what?" Aaron and Purr asked together.

"The Time-Warp-Turbo-History-5772-XL," she repeated. "I think that's the right name. It's kind of hard to remember." She picked it up and turned it over to see if the name was on it somewhere, then gently put it down.

Aaron leaned over to take a look. It had a flat screen the size of a notebook, with a small keyboard at the bottom.

"Dad made it out of recycled pieces of old computers and microchips. Not only is it the world's fastest computer, but you can type in any famous event in history, then tap the screen twice and you'll actually be able to watch the actual people doing the actual things they were actually doing at that actual moment," she said proudly. "Isn't that amazing?"

"Actually, I think catching a bug on the ceiling is way more amazing," said Purr, annoyed that she wasn't the most amazing one there.

"And what's even more amazing," Rabbi Mensch continued, "is that if you tap the screen three times, whatever you're watching will pop up so you can see it in 3D!"

"That's awesome!" Aaron exclaimed.

"I can dig up the living room plant in 3D. Now that's awesome," Purr chimed in, unimpressed.

"Dad is going to show everyone at the seder important Tu Bishvat events in the past," Rabbi Mensch said, ignoring her. "First we'll see the *Tree of Knowledge of Good and Bad* when *Adam and Eve* were in the *Garden of Eden* because that is believed to be the first tree created on Tu Bishvat. Then we'll watch rabbis having the first Tu Bishvat seder to thank G-d for nature, in a town called *Sfat* in the 16th century. Dad will even show us people planting trees in *Israel* after it became a country in 1948."

Aaron was stunned.

"Allow me to demonstrate," his mother said. She typed in "Garden of Eden." Then she moved her finger around the screen until she found Adam and Eve. She tapped three times. A miniature Adam and Eve popped up behind some bushes.

"Can I touch them?" Aaron asked, moving his finger in their direction.

"No!" she shouted, quickly pressing a yellow button that made them vanish. "The one big danger with this machine is that we can never, ever do anything that might change history. If we do, we could all disappear. The only reason we're here today is because everything that came before us occurred exactly the way it did."

"Aw, man," Aaron moaned. He was dying to touch some historical figures. "Hey, can we dive in there and hide behind a tree and watch stuff happening?"

"That would be way too dangerous," Rabbi Mensch replied, shaking her head. "If anyone saw us, or if we touched anything and changed history – poof!"

"And whatever you do," she said, even more seriously, "never, ever, ever, ever, ever tap the screen four times. I'm not sure what would happen, but whatever it is, Dad said it would be a total disaster."

"Yikes!" replied Aaron, jumping back.

"I promised Dad I would finish charging the battery," she continued. "But I guess it's OK if you keep watching it."

Aaron leaned over, with his hands behind his back to make sure he didn't touch anything. Adam and Eve were running frantically through the Garden.

"I wish I knew what just happened," he sighed, squinting to try to see further into the Garden of Eden.

CHAPTER THREE

TU BISH SWAT

Rabbi Mensch glanced at the kitchen clock. "Oy. Look at the time. We've got to get ready to go to the temple," she exclaimed.

"OK," said Aaron, hurrying upstairs behind her.

As soon as they were gone, Purr leaped back up onto the Time-Warp-Turbo-History-5772-XL. She stepped on a few keys and curled up in a ball.

"No one tells Purr what to do," she muttered, closing her eyes.

She began to have her favorite dream about chasing squirrels around the backyard.

Suddenly she felt something lumpy squirming under her tummy.

"Stop, that tickles," Purr said. She giggled in her sleep, thinking that a squirrel was playing with her.

"*Stp, tht tckls,*" a muffled voice squeaked from under Purr's fur.

"Huh?" Purr cried, opening one eye and realizing that there actually was something moving underneath her.

"*Hh?*" cried the lump, realizing that the thing on top of it wasn't just a ball of fur.

"Yikes!" Purr screamed, jumping up and looking beneath her. There was a shriveled piece of fruit, slightly bigger than a raisin, wearing little brown glasses. It had tiny arms and a stem on top. It looked

like a chunk was missing from each of its sides, giving it a stylish figure.

"*Yks!*" it squeaked, staring up at Purr's big face. It leapt off the screen and bounced onto the floor.

"Get back here," Purr shouted, bounding after it.

"*Dn't tch Tooty Fruity!*" it squeaked, bouncing across the kitchen. It banged into the wastebasket, toppling it onto Purr. Wrappers, old food and other garbage spilled all over her.

"*Y,y,y.y,y!*" it shrieked, bouncing back and forth.

"I'll get you for this, you tooty whatever your name is," yelled Purr from inside the wastebasket.

"I hope you're not making a mess down there," shouted Rabbi Mensch from the top of the stairs.

"Not me," Purr screeched. She suddenly realized that it wasn't so bad being stuck in a wastebasket. She shook off some stale pizza crusts and orange peels and began chewing on old chicken bones.

Tooty Fruity jumped onto the windowsill and noticed smoke coming out of the chimney.

It bounced up to the thermostat and turned down the heat.

"Gvlt, gvlt, gvlt," it squeaked in its tiny shrill voice.

Tooty zoomed around the room flicking off every light switch.

"Stp wstng ntr," it shrieked.

Then it jumped onto the sink and turned the handle until the faucet stopped dripping.

"What are you doing down there?" yelled Aaron as he emerged from the bathroom wrapped in a towel.

"Just getting a little snack," Purr shouted while licking the inside of an old tuna fish can.

Purr tipped the wastebasket on its side and backed out, smacking her lips. As Tooty Fruity ran by, she swatted it with her paw.

"Bd, bd, bd," it scolded, butting her paw with the tiny stem on its head.

"Ouch!" yelled Purr. "No piece of fruit is going to poke Purr and get away with it." She chased it back toward the trash can. At the last second, Tooty jumped to the side. But Purr couldn't stop in time. She charged inside so quickly that the wastebasket flipped into an upright position, trapping her in the bottom.

Tooty Fruity jumped back up onto the Time-Warp-Turbo-History-5772-XL. "Gt me bck to th Grdn," it yelled, bouncing around the screen.

When nothing happened, it started jumping on different keys. It typed:


```
Gt Tooty Fruity bck to th
        Grdn!!!
```


Then it hopped back on the screen.

Once again, nothing happened.

Purr freed herself from the wastebasket and took a running leap onto the table. Tooty Fruity screamed and dived into the bowl of raisins for cover.

"Get back here, you tooty fruitcake," she growled, sniffing around inside the bowl.

CHAPTER FOUR

TU BISH GOT TO GT BCK TO TH GRDN

Aaron fumbled down the stairs dressed in his temple clothes.

"Who turned out the lights?" he asked.

"And why is it so cold?" asked Rabbi Mensch, shivering behind him.

As Aaron turned on the light in the kitchen, Purr once again had her head in the bowl of raisins. Her back end was up in the air and her tail was wagging furiously.

"I'm gonna get that rotten Tooty Fruity," she grumbled.

"Those are raisins, not tooty fruities. And they certainly are not cat food," Aaron reminded her. "They're not rotten, just a little wrinkly."

Rabbi Mensch surveyed the mess on the kitchen floor. "Purr, I'm going to have to take away your Cat TV for the rest of the day," she scolded. "How many times do I have to tell you to leave the garbage alone?"

"At least she didn't touch the Time-Warp-Whozeewhatsit," said Aaron, more concerned about Dad's invention than anything else. "Hey. Why is the screen all lit up?"

"I don't know. That usually only happens if someone was just using it," Mom replied, glancing at Purr with a worried look. She quickly pressed the red button to turn it off and then unplugged it.

Aaron and Rabbi Mensch put on their winter coats.

"Please grab the bowl of raisins so you can hold them in the car," Rabbi Mensch requested. "I'll put the Time-Warp-Thingee-Dingee in my pocketbook."

As Aaron lifted the bowl, he thought he heard something squeak, "Gt me bck to th Grdn."

"What?" he asked, holding the bowl to his ear.

"I hope you didn't bury one of your toys in there," he warned Purr.

"Never in my wildest dreams," Purr replied, glaring at the bowl.

Aaron and his mom rushed out the door and into the car.

As soon as they started driving up the street, Rabbi Mensch's stomach began to growl. "I'm always in such a hurry that I never remember to eat," she mumbled. "I'm starving."

"Want a raisin?" asked Aaron from the back seat. "I'd like one, too."

"I guess we can each have one. Make mine the biggest one you can find," she told him.

Aaron searched through the bowl. He couldn't see too well because it was getting dark outside. But one of them did look bigger than the rest, even though it was pretty thin around the middle.

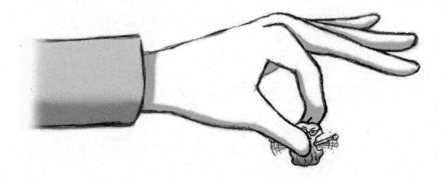

"I think this is the best one," he said, picking up Tooty Fruity by its face and handing it to his mother.

"Thanks," said Rabbi Mensch, reaching her hand behind her. She quickly popped it into her mouth and put her hand back on the steering wheel.

"Oy vy!" howled Tooty Fruity as two big rows of teeth started to close in on it.

Rabbi Mensch was so startled that she swallowed it whole.

"Are you all right, Aaron?" she asked, gagging a little. She didn't realize that the voice had come from her own mouth.

"I was going to ask you the same thing," he replied, with a worried look.

"Did that raisin you gave me fall on the floor?" she asked, sticking out her tongue. "It tastes like dust."

As soon as they stopped at a traffic light, she grabbed a plastic water bottle from the passenger seat to take a drink.

"Dn't use plstc!" shouted Tooty Fruity, swinging inside Rabbi Mensch's throat.

"You're absolutely right, Aaron. I should have a reusable water bottle in the car, particularly on Tu Bishvat when we celebrate nature," she replied.

"I agree," Aaron responded, confused. "But I didn't just say that."

Before she had time to think or drink, the traffic light turned green and they continued up the road to the temple.

"Please remind me to get gas on the way home," she said.

"*By n elctrc cr,*" shouted Tooty Fruity. "*Usng gs hrts th atmsphr.*"

"I love the way you're always thinking of ways to help the environment," she said, praising Aaron.

"Thanks but that wasn't me talking," Aaron replied. He looked all around the car trying to figure out what was going on as they drove into the temple parking lot.

CHAPTER FIVE

THE TU BISH PLOT THICKENS

Aaron's job was to set the long table for the temple seder. He unfolded the white paper tablecloths and set the table with the white paper plates he found in the temple kitchen. He took the stack of green paper cups and put one behind each plate. Then he added a *seder booklet* at each place.

As Rabbi Mensch rushed around to put out all the bowls of fruit, she began to have a funny feeling in her throat. Tooty Fruity tried to hang on tighter so it wouldn't fall off.

"*Sv th trs. Dn't use ppr,*" it shouted.

"But I thought that's what the paper supplies were here for," Aaron complained. He started to remove the cups and plates.

"What are you doing?" his mother asked, unaware that she had just said anything. "People are arriving and taking their seats. Why are you un-setting the table?"

"But you just told me not to use ppr," Aaron said. He thought for a moment. "Oh, I get it. You told me not to use pepper. Why would I put out pepper?" He grumbled as he put back all the paper products.

"Pepper has nothing to do with Tu Bishvat," Rabbi Mensch remarked, shaking her head.

She placed purple and white grape juice and purple and white wine on the tables. During the seder, everyone would make four different colored drinks in honor of the four seasons of the year – white for winter, pink for spring, red for summer and purple for fall.

Suddenly she felt like she had a sore throat.

"Just my luck." She moaned, grabbing her neck. "I hope I don't get sick right before the service."

"Are you OK?" asked Aaron.

When she opened her mouth to answer him, Tooty Fruity screamed from her throat, *"Hlp me! I cn't hld on mch lngr!"*

"What?" Aaron asked, shaking with fear. "Do you want me to call the doctor? Why are you talking so funny?"

"I don't know why I just said that," Rabbi Mensch replied. Her throat hurt but she didn't think she felt that bad.

She swallowed hard. Tooty swung into the sinus passage at the back of her throat, just in time.

"That's better," she said, sighing with relief.

As Aaron scooped out cupfuls of raisins and poured them into small paper bowls, a muffled voice shouted from inside his mother's head, *"Yr dstryng ntr! Dn't use ppr."*

"Did you say I was destroying nature?" he asked, getting frustrated. "And why do you keep telling me not to use pepper?"

There was so much noise that Rabbi Mensch didn't even hear herself or Aaron this time. Aaron plopped himself down on a chair at the head of the table and folded his arms. He was offended that after all his hard work, his mother kept yelling at him for things he didn't do.

Dad rushed in just before the seder was about to begin. He sat next to Aaron who whispered something in his ear. Dad looked at Rabbi Mensch with concern.

She handed Dad his invention. "I have the strangest itch behind my nose," she muttered.

The *cantor* joined them as they prepared to begin the service.

Rabbi Mensch stood to face the crowd. "Welcome to our Tu Bishvat seder to honor the New Year of the Trees and to thank G-d for nature," she announced, rubbing the top of her nose. "We begin with the opening song on page one, 'Let's Plant a Tree for Tu Bishvat.'"

The cantor looked at her as everyone opened their seder booklets. "O my G-d!" he gasped. "Are you OK?"

"The inside of my nose was a little itchy before, but it's fine now," Rabbi Mensch replied, giving him a weird look.

"But Rabbi, there's a huge lump rolling around inside your forehead," the cantor whispered in shock.

"What?" She put her hand up to her forehead and felt a huge rolling lump.

She bit her lip so she wouldn't scream. After all, 100 people were all staring at them, waiting to sing the opening song.

"Actually, the cantor is going to teach you a whole bunch of songs about Tu Bishvat," she announced as calmly as possible, pretending to scratch her forehead. "I'll be back in a moment."

The cantor began to panic. He knew that it might take her a while to come back. He searched his memory for all the nature songs he could think of.

CHAPTER SIX

TU BISH NOT

R abbi Mensch put her hand on her forehead, pretending to be deep in thought. She hurried out of the room, motioning to Dad and Aaron to follow her.

When they reached her office and closed the door behind them, Dad leaned in for a closer look.

"I've never seen anything like it," he exclaimed.

"Sorry, Mom, but it looks really funny." Aaron laughed as he watched the lump roll back and forth.

Dad powered up his Time-Warp-Turbo-History-5772-XL and frantically searched for information.

Meanwhile, Tooty Fruity rolled into Rabbi Mensch's ear. It banged on her eardrum and screamed, *"Gt me bck to th Grdn bfr it's too lt!"*

"What?" yelled Rabbi Mensch, grabbing her ear. "I don't even understand what you're saying."

"Who are you talking to? I didn't hear anything," said Dad, looking worried as he tried to figure out what was happening.

"The lump on Mom's forehead is gone," Aaron observed.

"Wait a second," Aaron continued, putting two and two together. "Let's call Purr. There seemed to be a lot of strange things happening in the kitchen while we were upstairs. I bet she knows something about this."

He thought some more and moaned. "Purr wouldn't stop staring at the bowl of raisins when we were about to leave. And I gave Mom a really strange looking raisin to eat on the car ride over.

"Mom said it tasted like dust," he added. "And Purr had dumped trash all over the kitchen floor."

Dad called Purr on her iCat. The phone rang and rang. Finally her answering machine came on.

THIS IS PURR. I'M TOO BUSY TO TALK TO YOU FRUITCAKES RIGHT NOW...

"Purr!" Dad shouted. "Pick up the phone. It's an emergency!"

Purr pressed the speaker button with her tail. "Don't bug me. I'm right in the middle of playing Mario Mouse," she griped.

"Was there something strange about the bowl of raisins?" asked Dad, ignoring her comment. "Mom swallowed one and it's rolling around inside her head."

"Well I was trying to take a cat nap on your dumb old thingamajigee and some annoying piece of fruit called Tooty Fruity popped out and poked me," Purr whined. "Gotta go or I'll never catch the rat and get to level 3!" Click.

"What?" yelled Dad. He checked the memory on his time machine. He saw Eve bite into a piece of fruit, then hand it to Adam. Adam took a bite, looked at Eve and screamed. He threw the fruit into the air. It landed in a big pile of dust. Sparks started flying out of it as it began to shake. Then the fruit disappeared and the screen went blank.

"The only reason why the screen would go blank is if something changed history at that moment," he explained. "And that could only happen if someone tapped the screen four times and made something from the past pop out."

"Owwwww," cried Rabbi Mensch as Tooty Fruity crashed into her cheekbone. Then it turned around and ran back into her sinuses.

"I'm glad I built in a 180 minute escape clause," Dad said, sighing with relief. "We've got 180 minutes from the time it popped out to get it back in there before the entire world disappears."

"Only 180 minutes?" moaned Rabbi Mensch, grabbing her nose. "To save the entire world?"

"Well actually it's 180 minutes from the time it popped out," Dad said, getting nervous. "How long ago was that?"

"Oy," groaned Rabbi Mensch, finding it hard to think with a piece of fruit in her head. "All I remember is that it was 5 o'clock when Aaron and I ran upstairs to get ready."

"Purr must have jumped on Dad's machine after we went upstairs. It's 7:30 now," Aaron said, checking the clock in Mom's office. "That's two and a half hours ago. That's … 150 minutes. That means we only have… 30 minutes left to get it out of Mom and back into the time machine before we all disappear!"

"How are we going to do that?" asked Rabbi Mensch, starting to get a really bad headache. "I'm the only one with superpowers, but I can't jump into myself! And Purr is home playing Mario Mouse."

CHAPTER SEVEN

TU BISH HOT SHOT

Aaron had a great idea. "Mom, remember that Rabbi Rocketpower Junior outfit you got me for Hanukkah? Remember how you always say that I'm your superboy in training? Could I please be the one to go into your head and get it out?" he pleaded.

"I'm sure you would do a wonderful job," his mother said. She groaned as Tooty Fruity slid behind her left eyeball. "But there's hardly any time left, so we would need someone who can catch things quickly to help you."

They all had the same idea. "Purr!" they shouted.

Rabbi Mensch began to spin like a pistachio. In seconds she transformed herself into the all-powerful Rabbi Rocketpower, who could do anything except jump into herself. She was wearing her blue outfit with a white *Jewish star* with an "R" on the front and her *tallis*-like cape on her back.

"Oy vay! Up, up and away!" she cried, vanishing into thin air. In a flash she returned with Purr squirming in her arms.

"I should have known you birdbrains couldn't handle this by yourselves. You're just lucky I was in the mood for a snack," said Purr, licking her lips.

"Let's go!" shouted Aaron, ready to spin.

"Hold on a second," said Rabbi Rocketpower, putting her hand on his shoulder. "Do you realize I'm going to have to shrink you so that you are so tiny that we will barely be able to see you?"

Aaron and Purr nodded excitedly.

"Do you promise to be really careful? I have to go back and lead the service while you're running around inside my body."

"No problem," said Aaron with a big smile and Purr with a big smirk.

"And do you realize that if we don't get the fruit back where it belongs in the next 27 minutes, we'll all disappear?" she asked, checking the clock with her one good eye.

"Do you realize that if you don't stop giving us warnings, we'll never be able to get in there and catch it?" asked Purr, rolling her eyes.

"Mom, is this right?" asked Aaron, spinning faster and faster. He turned into a superboy wearing his brand new outfit that had a big blue "A" in a Jewish star on the front.

Rabbi Mensch shrunk them to the size of pomegranate seeds. She quickly handed them to Dad then spun back into her normal self.

Aaron grabbed Purr. "Oy vay! Up, up and away!" he shouted, raising his free arm as he flew toward Rabbi Mensch's face.

They disappeared up her nose.

"Yuuuuuck!" they both shouted.

"Ugh," uttered Rabbi Mensch, trying not to scrunch up her nose as she felt them fly up it.

"Down to 25 minutes and 18 seconds," Dad whispered as he and Rabbi Mensch walked back into the social hall. She smiled, pretending that everything was fine. But as she walked up to the cantor, she sneezed. A tiny fur ball flew out of her nose and hit him in the forehead. He was so exhausted from singing every song he could think of having to do with a fruit or vegetable that he didn't notice.

CHAPTER EIGHT

TU BISH TROT

Suddenly something slid under Rabbi Mensch's chin. "G-d help me!" she exclaimed.

"I'm glad you're ready to pray," the cantor joked, rubbing his eye.

She asked the congregation to fill their cups with white grape juice or wine for the first season of winter. She began to feel something wriggle down her neck and into her shoulder blade.

"Please rise for the *Kiddush* over the first cup of wi-iiiiiiiiiii-ne," she blurted out, wiggling her right shoulder."

"Are you OK?" whispered the cantor.

"Perfectly fine," she assured him. But just as he was about to chant the Kiddush, Aaron and Purr chased Tooty Fruity toward Rabbi Mensch's stomach. She let out a loud burp.

"Pardon me," she apologized. The people sitting up front gave her a funny look.

The cantor sang and she began to take a sip of wine. But she realized that if she drank anything at all, Aaron and Purr would be washed into her stomach. She quickly put down her cup.

"We now continue with the first blessing over fru-hoo-hoo-hoo-hoot you can pe-he-he-he-heel." She screamed with laughter as a tiny tail tickled her under her right arm. She tried not to let anyone see her scratch her armpit. But the temple president who was sitting to her right looked at her with disapproval.

As everyone sat down to eat their oranges and almonds, Dad leaned over and whispered nervously

~ 45 ~

into Rabbi Mensch's ear, "only eighteen minutes left."

"Can you hear me in there?" he said more loudly into her nose.

The cantor looked at him as if he were nuts, but decided to focus on just making it through the seder.

"Let's continue with the pink cup of wine in honor of spring," Rabbi Mensch suddenly announced before people were done eating. She stood and raised her cup just as Tooty Fruity zigzagged into her brain.

But instead of reciting the Kiddush, she shouted, "*Stp dstryng ntr! Gt bck to th Grdn!*" and began bouncing up and down really fast. She would have spilled the wine if the cantor hadn't grabbed her cup.

"This is the best Tu Bishvat seder I've ever been to," five-year-old Danielle said to her mother. "Rabbi Mensch is so funny. I can't understand a word she's saying."

Rabbi Mensch looked at the little girl and smiled. But then Purr charged into her brain after Tooty Fruity.

"Get out of here, you doofus!" Rabbi Mensch screeched, grabbing her head.

"Mommy," Danielle cried. "Why did Rabbi Mensch say that to me?"

"I don't know," said her mother, giving Rabbi Mensch a dirty look.

Then Aaron ran into Rabbi Mensch's brain.

Suddenly she looked up and began waving and shouted, "Hi Mom! I'm in here!"

Everyone turned and looked to the back of the room, thinking that Rabbi Mensch's mother had just arrived for the seder.

While no one was looking, Rabbi Mensch put her hand over her mouth and whispered, "Aaron, Purr and whatever you are, get out of me this instant!"

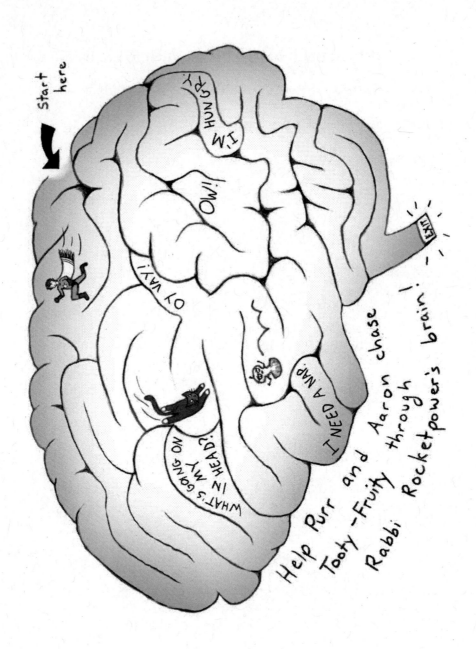

"Twelve minutes," Dad reported into her ear.

"Are you sure you're all right?" the cantor whispered in her other ear. By now he was totally bewildered by the rabbi's behavior.

After everyone saw that Rabbi Mensch's mother had not, in fact, entered the room, they looked back at her, not knowing what to think.

CHAPTER NINE

AH..AH..AH..CHOO BISHVAT

Rabbi Mensch stood up and raised her *Kiddush cup* so fast that a few drops of wine flew into the air.

"And now," she said, "please fill your cups with the purple wine or grape juice for fall so we can recite the fourth and final Kiddush."

"What happened to the third cup for summer?" asked Danielle's brother Ariel.

"Aren't we going to get to eat the fruit with pits and the fruit we can eat all of?" complained Danielle's other brother Nathaniel.

Before Rabbi Mensch could think of an excuse, Aaron and Purr pounced on Tooty Fruity as it ran toward the top of Rabbi Mensch's nose. "Ehhhh!" they cried as they began to slide down her nasal passage.

Rabbi Mensch's nose began to twitch. She felt like she was going to sneeze the biggest sneeze she had ever sneezed in her entire life.

"This last Kiddush is in honor of the fah, fah, fah, fah, fah, fah, fah … fall-choo!"

She sneezed so hard that Aaron, Purr and Tooty Fruity flew out of her nose toward the middle of the seder table.

"Yeowwww!" they cried in a chorus of high squeaky voices.

Dad quickly tried to aim the Time-Warp-Turbo-History-5772-XL at Tooty Fruity as it passed by in midair. He pressed the silver return button to suck it back into the machine and return it to the Garden of Eden.

But it was moving too fast.

Before you could say, "What's the name of that crazy contraption again?" Aaron and Purr disappeared into Dad's machine along with Tooty Fruity. As Dad frantically searched for the reverse button, he didn't realize he was aiming it at everyone who was sitting in front of him. Before anyone knew what was happening, people all over the social hall began flying toward him and out of sight.

By the time Dad remembered that he had forgotten to build in a reverse button, there was no one left in the room except for Rabbi Mensch and the cantor. Lucky for them, they happened to be the only ones standing behind him.

They looked into the screen. There was the whole congregation chasing Aaron through the Garden of Eden. The temple president was shouting, "Come back! We have to finish the seder . . . hmm, these fruit trees are beautiful."

Aaron was chasing Purr, screaming, "Leave Tooty Fruity alone! Wow. The air smells really clean here."

Purr was chasing Tooty Fruity, yelling, "Get back here . . . mmm, look at all these yummy bugs."

Tooty Fruity was bouncing after Adam and Eve, shrieking, *"Ppl r dstryng th erth bcause you ate me!"*

Adam and Eve were running around the Tree of Knowledge of Good and Bad, crying, "What did we do? What did we do?"

"Oy vay," uttered Dad. "Tooty Fruity must have been the fruit Adam and Eve ate from the Tree of Knowledge of Good and Bad."

"That's why it was smart enough to figure out all the bad things we are doing to nature," Rabbi Mensch realized. "Since it's from the Tree of Knowledge, it would know that paper products are made by cutting down trees, that pollution is caused by turning up the heat, having gas engines in our cars, and throwing away plastic containers."

"Can you imagine being in the Garden of Eden one day and in our world the next?" asked Dad, shaking his head. "It must have been shocked to see what people have done to the earth."

"How did it ever come to life?" Rabbi Mensch wondered. "And why does it speak with missing letters? And how did it ever pop out of the screen if no one tapped it four times?"

The cantor wasn't any help. So many crazy things had happened that all he could do was stare straight ahead with his mouth open.

"All I know is that if we don't put Tooty Fruity back where it was at the exact moment in history when it popped out and get everyone out of there in the next six minutes and eighteen seconds, we won't be around to figure out the answers," shouted Dad.

They looked back down at the screen. Now all they could see was a bunch of trees. They heard faint noises in the distance. Dad scrolled around the screen with his finger, desperately trying to find everyone.

"That's an awfully weird pile of dust next to the Garden," he observed. "There are sparks lighting it up."

"That must be the dust G-d blew into to make Adam," explained Rabbi Mensch. "Can you enlarge the picture?"

Dad zoomed in on the pile of dust. There was a little indentation on the top.

"Wait a second. Maybe that's where the fruit that Adam bit into landed after he threw it into the air. I bet that's why it tasted dusty," concluded Rabbi Mensch.

"And maybe it came to life because God's breath got inside of it through the places where it had been eaten," Dad added.

"And maybe it spoke with missing letters because it was missing parts of itself," Rabbi Mensch suggested. "But I still don't understand how it popped out of the machine."

"Three minutes left," Dad interrupted. "And now I can't even hear them in the distance."

"I knew I'd have to save the day somehow before this story was over," Rabbi Mensch exclaimed.

Before you could say, "Almost-Out-Of-Time-Warp-Turbo-History-5772-XL," she spun into Rabbi Rocketpower, faster than a speeding almond, more powerful than a pomegranate, able to save the day with a flick of her mighty *yad* and a blast from her trusty *shofar*.

"Oy vay! Up, up and away!" she shouted as she flew into the air and dived into the screen.

In no time at all, Rabbi Rocketpower located everyone in the Garden of Eden. She grabbed Tooty Fruity. As she zoomed toward the dust pile, she promised Tooty Fruity that she would try to get people to take better care of nature in the future.

"Too-da-loo," she cried as she placed Tooty Fruity in the indentation on the dust pile. She zapped it with her mighty yad so it wouldn't remember anything.

With no time to spare, Rabbi Rocketpower flew back to Adam and Eve, apologized for the rude interruption and zapped their memories so they wouldn't remember what just happened.

As Dad nervously watched the timer tick down to eighteen seconds, she blew her trusty shofar so loudly that it sent the entire congregation flying back to the seder. They all sat still in their seats, dazed. As the timer ticked down, five, four, three, two, one . . . Rabbi Rocketpower jumped out of the screen with Aaron under one arm and Purr under the other.

"No dumb piece of fruit annoys Purr and gets away with it," Purr griped. She kept complaining until Rabbi Rocketpower threatened to send her iCat back to the Garden of Eden.

Aaron grabbed Purr, sat back down at the table, and placed her on his lap. "Please be quiet while Mom finishes the seder," he whispered.

"Seder? Wake me up when it's over." Purr yawned and closed her eyes. As Rabbi Rocketpower made sure everyone was back in their seats, Purr began to snore. As she chased squirrels in her favorite dream, she began thumping her tail on Aaron's leg, once, twice, three times, then a fourth.

"I got it!" Aaron cried. "Purr must have wagged her tail four times while she was sleeping on Dad's computer majigee. I bet Tooty Fruity was on the screen at that second and that's why she popped out!"

"I should have known Purr was at the bottom of this," muttered Rabbi Rocketpower.

"Remind me never to leave my inventions lying around the house," said Dad, grabbing his head.

CHAPTER TEN

TU BISH TAUGHT

Rabbi Rocketpower waved her mighty yad around the room to wake everyone up from their daze as she finished spinning back into Rabbi Mensch.

She tried to explain what happened with Tooty Fruity and the Garden of Eden. Everyone continued to stare straight ahead.

"Well, I certainly learned a lot more about Tu Bishvat this year than I expected," she continued with a chuckle.

"I learned that like the peel protects the inside of an orange, Tooty Fruity helped to remind us that we need to protect the earth against pollution. It's amazing how much of the earth has been destroyed since the Garden of Eden because people didn't take care of it."

Everyone nodded, but stared into space.

"I learned that like the date has a hard pit inside, we need to have a strong heart like our friend Tooty Fruity. It was in a foreign place and an unfamiliar time. But it was brave enough to keep telling us an extremely important message, that nature will be destroyed if we don't change the way we treat it."

Everyone nodded again, like zombies.

"And just like the raisin that we can eat all of, we all need to follow Tooty Fruity's example to make the world a better place. Before we end our seder, let's think about how wonderful the world was in the days of the Garden of Eden," Rabbi Mensch suggested.

"If we each promise to clean up the earth in one specific way, we can help nature get back to the way it was on the very first Tu Bishvat. Do you agree?"

Everyone nodded again in silence.

"Great. Now it's time for us to eat all the delicious fruits and nuts that connect us with Israel–the almonds, the oranges, the figs, the dates, the pomegranates, the olives, and the raisins."

No one moved.

"Um, Rabbi," mumbled the cantor. "I don't think anyone feels like eating after what just happened."

"Well then," said Rabbi Mensch. "Let's just skip to our closing song, 'Aytz Haim Hee,' 'It is a Tree of Life.'"

"Not again," groaned Danielle.

"Didn't we already sing that one?" asked Ariel.

"About 15 times at the beginning of the service," said Nathaniel.

"Think of it as a great way to recycle," the cantor replied.

As everyone began to sing, Rabbi Mensch, Aaron and Dad sighed with relief, while Purr pouted on Aaron's lap.

Another holiday. Another adventure.

HOW TO PLOT A TU BISHVAT SEDER

What To Have On the Seder Table:

Bottles of white & purple grape juice and/or wine

Fruit with shells (oranges, clementines, pomegranates, almonds, walnuts, pecans, carob, bananas)

Fruit with pits (dates, olives, peaches, apricots, cherries, plums, avocados)

Entirely edible fruit (figs, grapes, raisins, berries)

To make it even more special, you could have 15 types of fruit in honor of the 15th day of the month, and something made out of wheat and barley (two of the seven species G-d promised the Israelites when they came to the land of Israel).

Each Person Needs:

Kiddush cup

Plate

Tu Bishvat seder booklet – Tu Bishvat seders may be found on the Internet. Or you can email Rabbi Rocketpower (author@rabbirocketpower.com) and she will email you the actual seder she uses at her actual temple.

TU BISH BARK

Only make this recipe if there is an adult there to help.

Ingredients
3 cups chocolate (whatever kind you like, depending on your taste preferences and if you would like it to be dairy or pareve)

1½ - 2 cups of any or all of your favorite fruit and nuts (diced dried apricots, raisins, toasted slivered almonds, cranberries, pomegranate seeds, diced dried dates)

Directions
1. Melt chocolate in a pot over very low heat on the stove, stirring until smooth. You can also microwave it in a microwave-safe bowl, on half-power at 30-second intervals, stirring frequently until fully melted.

2. Add remaining ingredients, mixing well.

3. Line cookie sheets with wax paper.

4. Drop tablespoonfuls of the chocolate mixture onto the paper or make one giant piece of bark which you can break later.

5. Refrigerate until hardened (at least 30 minutes).

6. Remove from wax paper and place on plate.

Makes about 18 servings.

This recipe can also be found online at www.ShalomBoston.com.

15 TU-RIFIC WAYS TO SAVE THE PLANET

Have a reusable water bottle.

Eat locally grown food.

Light your house with energy efficient bulbs.

Promise to recycle.

Reuse your lunch box.

Only keep the TV on while you are watching it.

Conserve water.

Keep the lights off when you're not in a room.

Eat more veggies, less meat.

Turn off the computer at night.

Plant trees, herbs, fruit or vegetables.

Organize a neighborhood or park clean-up.

Walk, or ride a bike.

Enter writing and art contests to spread this message.

Read about environmental issues.

For more ideas check out the Coalition on the Environment and Jewish Life, www.coejl.org.

GLOSSARY

Adam and Eve – The first two human beings according to the Torah. The Torah tells us that Eve was made from Adam's rib because he got lonely being in the Garden all by himself. Eve was the first one to take a bite out of the fruit from the Tree of Knowledge. Uh-oh. The rest is history.

Cantor – The person who leads the singing at a Jewish worship service. Cantors also teach and lead all kinds of Jewish ceremonies.

Garden of Eden – The special place G-d put Adam and Eve so they could take care of it and have all the yummy fruit they wanted. Too bad about what happened there.

Israel –The homeland of the Jewish people. Today it is a modern country. Have you ever been there? You should plan on going sometime. You can see a lot of places mentioned in the Torah.

Jewish Star – A six-pointed star. Also known as *Magen David* which means Shield of David because King David used this symbol on his shield. It is so important that it is even on the middle of the flag of the State of Israel. Can you draw one? All you need to do is make two triangles on top of each other, one pointing up and one pointing down. Rabbi Rocketpower draws them whenever she doodles.

~ 71 ~

Kiddush – The Hebrew word for "to make holy." The name of the blessing over the wine. Do you remember why we say it four times during a Tu Bishvat seder?

Kiddush Cup – The special cup that you fill with wine or grape juice and hold up when you recite the Kiddush.

Seder – The Hebrew word for "order." We call a Tu Bishvat or Passover service a seder because there is a very specific order to how we do things.

Seder Booklet – Or Haggadah. The service that contains the prayers and blessings we recite.

Seven Types of Fruit – The seven species of fruit (and grains) which are mentioned in the Torah as the food G-d promises to give the Israelites when they enter the land of Israel. They are: wheat, barley, grapes, figs, pomegranates, olives, and dates.

Sfat – A town in northern Israel where Jewish mystics lived in the 16th century. One of Rabbi Rocketpower's favorite places. If you ever go to Israel, definitely plan on visiting.

Shofar – A ram's horn that Jews blow to announce the Jewish New Year (Rosh Hashanah) and the end of the Day of Atonement (Yom Kippur). Some people also use it to announce that Shabbat is coming. It makes a very powerful sound, but it's really hard to do. Try it!

Shvat - The fifth month of the Hebrew year. It always comes around January or February. Bet you can't name all the Hebrew months!

Tallis – The prayer shawl Jews wear when they lead a worship service or when they pray during the day. It makes you feel special when you wear one, like being wrapped in a prayer or hugged by G-d. Only adults are supposed to wear them. But you could still try one on.

Temple – The building where Jews meet to worship, study and get together. It is also called a synagogue or a shul. They can be as big as a school or as small as a little house. The original Temple was in Jerusalem.

Tree of Knowledge of Good and Bad – The only tree in the Garden of Eden which Adam and Eve were not supposed to eat from. But wouldn't you know it, that was the one whose fruit the serpent convinced them to taste. Extremely bad idea. If someone tries to convince you to do something you know is wrong, don't do it!!!!!

Tu Bishvat – The fifteenth day of the Hebrew month of Shvat. The name of the New Year of the Trees, since that is the day all trees in Israel are considered to be one year older. It is the beginning of spring, when the almond trees start to blossom in Israel. Many people also celebrate this holiday by planting trees in Israel. Great idea! You should try it. Just contact the Jewish National Fund (www.jnf.org).

Tu Bishvat Seder – The special service we have to honor the New Year of the Trees. This ceremony began a really long time ago by a group of mystical people in a town in northern Israel called Sfat. We drink four cups of grape juice or wine in honor of each of the four seasons. We eat three types of fruit. But you probably know all this already from reading the book.

Time-Warp-Turbo-History-5772-XL – Dad's craziest, most amazing invention ever. It gives you a 3D view into any time in history you want to see. But whatever you do, NEVER tap the screen four times.

Yad – The Hebrew word for "hand." It's also the name of the pointer you use when you read out of the Torah scroll so you won't touch it with your fingers, since it is a holy object. Rabbi Rocketpower's yad has superpowers. When you read out of the Torah using a yad, you will feel like you have superpowers too.

GLSSRY

Bd, bd, bd. – Bad, bad, bad.

By n elctrc cr. – Buy an electric car.

Dn't tch Tooty Fruity! – Don't touch Tooty Fruity!

Dn't use plstc! – Don't use plastic!

Gt me bck to th Grdn bfr it's too lt! – Get me back to the Garden before it's too late!

Gvlt, gvlt, gvlt – Gevalt, gevalt, gevalt *(another way to say "oy vay" or "oh no!")*

Hh? – Huh?

Hlp me! I cn't hld on mch lngr! – Help me! I can't hold on much longer!

Ppl r dstryng th erth bcause you ate me! – People are destroying the earth because you ate me!

Stp dstryng ntr! Gt bck to th Grdn! – Stop destroying nature! Get back to the Garden!

~ 75 ~

Stp wstng ntr! – Stop wasting nature!

Stp, tht tckls. – Stop, that tickles.

Sv th trs. Dn't use ppr. – Save the trees. Don't use paper.

Usng gs hrts th atmsphr. – Using gas hurts the atmosphere.

Y,y,y,y,y! – Oy,oy,oy,oy,oy!

Yks! – Yikes!

Yr dstryng ntr! Dn't use ppr. – You're destroying nature! Don't use paper.

ACKNOWLEDGMENTS

This book would never have seen the light of day without the dedication, enthusiasm, and creativity of the Rabbi Rocketpower crew.

Laura Standley, our new illustrator, has dazzled us with her incredible talent. Though she is only a senior in high school, the quality of her work rivals that of seasoned professionals. Her creativity, sense of humor, eye for detail, and perfectionist nature have truly enriched the text.

Neither of us could have completed this task without the professional guidance, enthusiasm, and wonderful spirit of Susanna Natti, our Art Director. She generously gave us the gift of her wisdom, keen eye, sense of humor and expertise every step of the way.

Fran Bloomfield spent innumerable hours making sure every detail of this book was as grammatically accurate as possible. This was after she spent innumerable hours challenging me to develop the plot and the characters, and debating the humor of words, phrases, and situations. There were many late nights on the phone when we laughed ourselves silly.

Neither this book nor this series would exist without the kindness, support, and generosity of Carol Feltman, publisher, friend, and Rabbi Rocketpower fan. Thanks to Amanda and Rebecca Feltman for their suggestions and advice.

Lisa DiOrio, our high tech guru, has continued to maintain and update www.rabbirocketpower.com, our website, with creativity and expertise.

I appreciate all the efforts of Joan Perlman, our marketing maven, who has worked tirelessly to promote the Rabbi Rocketpower series.

Thank you to the following students of Temple Shalom Emeth's religious school for all their helpful comments and suggestions – Melissa Atkins, Sydney Cooperman, Jeremy Fox, Aviah Levine, Alyssa Porter, Aaron Rippin, Alia Weiner, and Cassidy Worrall and their teacher, Judy Apkin.

Finally, thank you to my son Aaron, without whom the idea for this book and this series would never have come to be. It was in 2001, when he was in the first grade at the Rashi School in Newton, MA, that we developed these stories as a fun way to experience the Jewish holidays together.

Rabbi Susan Abramson, D.D.

November 2011

The reviews are in:

Rabbi Rocketpower's <u>Who Hogged The Hallah?</u>,
<u>The Mystery of the Missing Menorahs</u> and
<u>The Half-Baked Matzah Mystery</u> are a blast!

* It was hilarious. I loved it and I hope you will too.
Ethan, age 11

* This book is funny and fun for young or older aged kids. Alex, age 10

*My daughter requested an immediate second reading. How amazingly creative to have a fun, suspenseful book with no bad elements.
Marjorie (mother of Sydney, age 5)

*It teaches about Hanukkah while reading the funny story. You should read this book.
Amanda, age 9

*When I was 7 years old, I read this story and I could even understand the big words in it. If you want to know more about the book, buy a copy! Rebecca, age 8

www.rabbirocketpower.com

Check out Rabbi Rocketpower on YouTube!

With an adult, search for "Rabbi Rocketpower" on YouTube.

Learn how to make challah with Rabbi Rocketpower herself:

"The Rabbi's Kitchen" Episode 1: A Beginner's Guide to Great Challah

"The Rabbi's Kitchen" Episode 2: How To Make High Holy Day Challah

Watch a cartoon video of <u>The Half-Baked Matzah Mystery</u>, read by Rabbi Rocketpower herself:

See the video Purr the Purreneal Pest, which Aaron made of Purr typing on the computer!